Education's
Not
The Point

Education's *Not* The Point

*Why Schools Fail to Train Children's Minds
and Nurture Their Characters*

*John Taylor Gatto
Dorothy L. Sayers
Elizabeth Y. Hanson*

© 2024 Lost Tools Press, LLC

Published by Lost Tools Press
8 The Greene, Suite 5604
Dover, DE 19901
www.losttoolspress.com

All right reserved. No part of this publication may be reproduced, stores in a retrieval system or transmitted in any form by any means, electronic, mechanical, photocopy, recording or otherwise, without the prior written permission of Lost Tools Press, LLC.

ISBN 978-0-9892800-5-1 (paperback)
ISBN 978-0-9892800-6-8 (EPUB)

Cover photo by Peter Sanders
© 2023 Peter Sanders Photography

Typography by Danny Nanos

Elizabeth Hanson initially published John Taylor Gatto's essay, *A Short Angry History of Compulsory Schooling*, with John's permission, in 2003. It is reprinted here under the revised book title *Education's Not the Point*.

Revised Version ©2003 John Taylor Gatto

For the children

Contents

A Short Angry History of Compulsory Schooling   1
John Taylor Gatto

The Lost Tools of Learning   41
Dorothy L. Sayers

Is a *Head* Start Damaging Our Children's *Hearts*?
Elizabeth Y. Hanson   73

"Getting better teachers, better principals, better superintendents, or better textbooks will not solve the school mess, to do that requires us to understand what forced schooling is really about and what we jeopardize by trying to rock its boat."

JOHN TAYLOR GATTO,
author of *Dumbing Us Down*

A Short Angry History of Compulsory Schooling

John Taylor Gatto

1.

THE MAN FROM whom I first got wind of the real purposes of American schooling was James Bryant Conant, one of the truly influential Americans of the 20th century. Dr. Conant, descendant of a Mayflower family, was president of Harvard for 30 years, a WWI poison gas specialist, a WWII inner-circle executive on the atomic bomb project, high commissioner of the American zone in occupied Germany after that war ended, and a pivotal figure in the evolution of American forced schooling, as you'll discover in a little while.

But first you and I must lay some groundwork before we can properly understand what official schooling is meant to be. And keep in mind as I speak about schooling that education and schooling are quite different things. Long-term schooling can only achieve its purposes by inflicting a profound degree of boredom on the young. I'll defend that thesis later, but for the moment fix your attention on the concept of *boredom*. If you went through 12 years of school, you were often bored.

I couldn't have been older than seven when my grandfather told me one day after I'd complained of being bored that I was never to say that word aloud again in his presence or he would slap me silly. He said that the obligation to amuse and instruct myself was entirely my own, the buck couldn't be passed to anyone else. He said that bored people were childish people, always to be avoided. Boredom and childishness are closely allied with one another; those trapped in both states have no clear idea of what to do with time, no wisdom about priorities.

2.

Think of institutional schooling as it has evolved over the past 100 years as a laboratory of extended childishness. In the act of having their childhood artificially extended, in ways they can feel, but lack the perspective to think about cogently, most schoolchildren are frequently bored. I want you to consider the possibility that these feelings have been evoked for some rational reason, and as you consider boredom as an essential part of the school equation, remember that institutionalized schoolteachers are bored, too—though they might not so readily admit to it.

I taught school for 30 years. From experience I can tell you that boredom is the common condition of schoolteachers: low energy, whining, and dispirited speech inside the teacher culture are readily observable signs of a hollow inner state, one waiting to be filled up by somebody else.

If you ask school kids, as I often did, *why* they feel so bored, they always give the same few answers. They say that the work is stupid, that it makes no sense, or that they already know it. They say they want to be doing something real, not just sitting around; they say the teachers don't seem to know much about their subjects and clearly aren't interested in what they teach.

And when you ask teachers why they are bored, they say it's the kids' fault. They say the kids are rude, that they aren't interested in anything except grades. So how can a teacher be interested in them? It's a Catch 22, you see.

When you spend some time watching schools, you gradually become aware of what childish places they are, that kids and teachers are held prisoners there in a childhood they would willingly have left long ago, if they knew how, and if the institution had encouraged them to escape that dependent condition.

Let's define terms a bit further before continuing. Visualize a continuum from childlike on one end to childish on the other. Childlike is what we *expect* young children to be; innocent, trusting, anxious to please, full of wonder, respectful. Childish is the dark other side of childlike, childish people are selfish, irresponsible, bored, envious, inconsiderate, whining. In general, childish people lack emotional proportion.

Now contrast these two terms with another familiar word —youthful. Can you sense immediately we are on different ground! Youthful offers quite a positive window on the early years. It suggests adventurousness, energy, curiosity, resilience, indomitability, the capacity to surprise, an openness to new experience.

Schooling could not exist in its customary shapes if it encouraged the qualities of youthfulness; literally, it could not contain them without exploding its structure. Is this not a strange institution then which finds itself compelled to suppress those very qualities of youthfulness which are widely acknowledged to be passports to success in Western society?

Since personal expression (and development) is so rigorously constrained by the structures of schooling—rigorously enough that youthfulness is suffocated (although childishness is nurtured)—a disinterested observer might be expected to hypothesize that some greater interest is being served by schools as they are, an interest which must be protected from the ingredients, and eventual outcomes, of youthful expression. Put another way, schools couldn't be the way they are, so expensively flying in the face of common sense and long experience in how children learn things, unless they were doing something right from some particular point of view. Schools may not seem reasonable places to me or to you—or to many children—but that's not to say they aren't, at all times, *rational* from where the managers of our society sit.

To belabor what seems to me obvious: schools wouldn't be as they are unless that suited the most important men and women in the world; obviously if schools *displeased* the managers of society, they would cease to exist as they are, over time. How, indeed, could it be otherwise? If we persist in thinking like engineers about the particular problems of schooling, like bad reading or bad manners, we will surely miss seeing what the school forest is really about, for concentrating too heavily on its trees. Getting better teachers, better principals, better superintendents, or better textbooks will not solve the school mess, to do that requires us to understand what forced schooling is really about —and what we jeopardize by trying to rock its boat.

3.

Secondary school was hardly the only path to maturity until after WWII. Junior high school didn't exist in many places until then and high school was only a part of the upbringing of a fraction of the young until well after the First World War. To give just two examples that I took very casually from *The New York Times* of 18 April, this year [2003], and the *New Yorker* magazine of April 21: in a Times obituary for the 101st richest man in the world, John S. Latsis, who built a global empire in shipping, I learned that he was born in 1910 in the Greek fishing village of Katakola where, virtually unschooled, he began his working life as a laborer before he graduated to being a deckhand on a freighter. At 28, with his savings and some loans, he bought a rusty freighter which, over the next three decades, he parlayed into a fleet of ships. He then, without any instruction, diversified into construction, oil, banking, and the like without even an MBA from the Harvard Business School. Over the years his yacht was lent to Prince Charles, to President George Bush, to Colin Powell, and to Marlon Brando. How's that for a Greek laborer without a college degree?

The other obit-profile I unearthed without any deliberate

research, on the same day I saw the *New York Times* piece, was about another fellow without a college degree. His name was Lew Wasserman and according to the *New Yorker* he was "the most significant player in the creation of the Hollywood that we know today."

Wasserman was born in 1913. By the age of 12 he was selling candy in a theatre and at fifteen he had a regular job, working as a movie usher from 3PM to midnight, seven days a week. He needed to miss high school to keep his job so he made deals, with the principal and the teachers: with the principal he agreed to raise enough money to pay for the school athletic uniforms (which he did by showing movies at the school for 3 cents an admission), with the chemistry teacher his attendance was waived if he passed the tests (which he did by studying on his own). So much for Wasserman's "education." He couldn't afford college, which was time saved for other things. Wasserman used the time to buy up the contracts of Greta Garbo, Fred Astaire, Henry Fonda, Billy Wilder, Josh Logan, Dorothy Parker, Dashiell Hammett, and others (using someone else's money, of course), and by the age of 33 he was president of M.C.A., the Music Corporation of America. He studied tax law on his own and invented a variety of structured transactions and deferred compensation plans which specialist attorneys had never thought of.

If biographies like this are news to you, it isn't your fault. Although 50 years ago schools commonly talked of these alternative route triumphs, they don't anymore; nor do America's important news outlets focus your attention on how many people make it without benefit of schooling. If you think I'm exaggerating, how many of you know that as I speak, across the ocean in wealthy Switzerland, less than one kid in four goes beyond elementary school? In the richest nation in the world, per capita, over 75 percent of the population has only a grade school background.

4.

Through most of American history, most kids didn't go to secondary school. Yet the unschooled rose to be admirals, like Farragut, inventors, like Edison; captains of industry, like Carnegie and Rockefeller; presidents, like Washington and Lincoln; fast-food tycoons like Ray Kroc of McDonald's or Dave Thomas of Wendy's; writers like Herman Melville or Joseph Conrad; scholars, like Margaret Meade. None of these names were ever sentenced to 12 years in a classroom.

For most of history, including our own history, people who reached the age of 13 weren't looked upon as children. Ariel Durant, who co-wrote an enormous multi-volume history of the world of which millions of copies are in American homes thanks to the Book-Of-The-Month Club, was happily married at the age of 15 to her co-author Will Durant, to whom she remained married for more than 50 years until his death. Will was 26, Ariel 15.

Would she really have been better off doing tenth grade homework than starting her life studying professional historiography. Something has been left out of the stories we've been sold about the proper role of fifteen-year olds, and to find out what that is I need to take you back to the foundry where childlike, childish, boring schools were fashioned—a northern European nation, now vanished, called Prussia.

By 1820, Prussia was teaching the important countries of the world that forced schooling could be a habit-training laboratory for obedient subjects, men and women whose responsiveness to political and economic exhortation could be counted upon. Thus was a novel "fourth purpose" for the school institution put into play; such a purpose had been conceived in antiquity—Plato wrote eloquently of such a system in his *Republic and Laws*—New England had briefly tried the idea without success in the 17th century, too, but the laurel of forced schooling must go to Prussia.

It was from Prussia that the idea and the method spread west and east, first to the United States and France, later to Britain and Japan and everywhere else. And the world was soon to learn over the course of three titanic Prussian wars, between 1871 and 1945, just how well this scheme worked to concentrate state power. As the psychologies, hard and soft, developed in Prussia and the other Germanies, it was seen that school could become a conditioning laboratory, making children susceptible to any sort of authoritarian command, including the soft-core authoritarianisms of advertising and public relations.

5.

If children could be trained to surrender their judgements and their free wills to political exhortations and commercial blandishments, a revolution in economic affairs would be at hand. In 1776 Adam Smith had detailed the implacable laws of supply and demand in his immortal essay, *The Wealth of Nations*, but suddenly Prussian schooling and German psychology opened a whole new world, one in which Adam Smith's laws could be repudiated by the clever. For if demand could be created for virtually any product and service, and for any political idea, then a managerial revolution was at hand. One which freed managers, (and after all politicians are our social managers, so them, too) from a slavish dependence on public opinion. With enough resources and enough access, public opinion could be what management wanted it to be.

Think of the business school subject loosely called "marketing." If people want something there is really little need to "market" it to them. Anyone can sell ice to Bombay as New England merchants proved two hundred years ago; it's selling ice to Eskimos or $150 sneakers to poor children when those sneakers are no better constructed than $15 bargain shop brands that takes the marketing. What marketing really means is overcoming sales resistance, regardless of the reasons for that resistance.

It's an art, but what if it could be made into a science? How? By isolating children far from the everyday world, by confining them with total strangers in strange, sterilized environments where various inputs could be studied, where growing children could be scrutinized, labeled and numbered for different future utilizations. And where data collected from these children could be passed on to other levels of authority for evaluation. Out of this flow of information, materials toward a science of marketing and a science of management would inevitably arise.

Prussian habit-control schooling was turned to serve the emerging mass production business empires, not all at once, of course, but bit by bit. Thus the founders of compulsion schooling aimed at collectivizing and socializing the ordinary population not by main force, not by bayonets or drillmasters, but through the inculcation of dependency habits in children. Bluntly put, this founding generation of institutional pedagogues executed a plan to extend childhood well beyond its natural limits. They arranged the removal of young people from home and neighborhood associations and their placement with a substratum of pedagogues who might be thought of as false kin, people utterly unknown to the children's parents. To deepen the estrangement, these strangers we call schoolteachers were often relatively ignorant and childish themselves. Virtually stripped of any effective authority, the teachers were under the comprehensive direction of faraway strangers, men and women who, in most cases, remained nameless and faceless to the teacher cadre.

Over time, students came to see that their teachers cringed at the approach of various school administrators; what they could not see was each level of administration cringed at the one above it: the principal cringed before the superintendent, the superintendent before many levels of authority—perhaps the principal local industries, perhaps the Carnegie Foundation, or the state education department, or one of the government agencies which appear and disappear regularly in the life of a school. And yet none of these agencies ordering about the lives of school superintendents is itself sovereign, each takes many of its marching orders from elsewhere, and to find out from where is not easy. Superintendents learn to sense where they must defer to others, they never learn why. And if they fail to defer they don't last long. In this amazing fragmentation of control resides the immense stability of institutional schooling—nobody knows how to get anything much done without breaking the law, written or unwritten.

6.

Over the course of the twentieth century, the original three purposes of schooling: 1) to make good people 2) to make good citizens and 3) to make each person his or her personal best gave way to the new Prussian "fourth purpose" everywhere. In the fourth purpose, kids are looked upon as "human resources" to be expended by the nation's managers when, where, and how they will do the most good for political, social, and economic efficiency. Lip service still was (and is) paid to the original purposes, but to the extent these attractive targets are excessively achieved, the entire system is thrown into peril. We have not evolved either a society or an economy which welcomes principled people, or noisy citizens, or too many accomplished, self-reliant people. At the corporate center of our economy, made possible by uniform forced schooling, principled people and noisy citizens are a deadly nuisance, one which threatens to violate chain-of-command authority unpredictably, and efficient systems do not depend upon accomplished, self-reliant employees, but on qualities quite different.

7.

At the beginning of my presentation, I told you that Dr. Conant, the long-time president of Harvard, the poison gas/atomic explosion specialist, was a pivotal figure in giving us the schools we got in the century just past. Without him, for example, we would be unlikely to have the style and degree of standardized testing which we enjoy (pardon my sarcasm), nor would we have the gargantuan high school plants which warehouse two to five thousand students—like the famous Columbine in Littleton, Colorado.

It was from Conant that I first got wind of the real purposes of American schooling. In a book he wrote published in 1949, bearing the title *The Child, the Parent, and the State*, Conant mentions in passing that the modern schools we attend were the result of a coup! "Coup" is Conant's word, not mine. I presume that when a Harvard president, let alone a fellow importantly responsible for Lewisite gas (or atomic bombs) uses a term like "coup", he means just that. Unfortunately, he fails to elaborate on any details in his book, but he does state that the curious and uninformed should pick up a book published in 1911 called *Principles of Secondary Education* in order to learn chapter and verse of the coup.

Eventually I was able to do that, but along the way I learned that the book's author, Alexander Inglis, (pronounced Ing-els, I believe), had been a Harvard professor back around the time of WWI, whose name is kept alive by having the honor lecture in education at Harvard named after him, "The Inglis Lecture." I learned also that Inglis came from a distinguished English family who fought on the British side in the American Revolution. One member wrote a refutation of Tom Paine's *Common Sense*, one tried to establish the Anglican faith, Britain's official religion, as the state faith of America as well. And later, another Inglis was the Commanding General at the siege of Lucknow in India during the Sepoy uprising in 1857—promoted to Major General for blowing the rebellious Sepoy wretches apart with his cannons.

According to Dr. Inglis, modern, institutionalized, compulsion-schooling has six functions, which I'll get to in a moment. But first he makes it clear that school on this continent was intended to be what it had been in northern Germany: a fifth column into the burgeoning libertarian/democratic condition in which the peasantries and proletariats clamored for some voice at the bargaining table.

School was to provide a surgical incision into the prospective unity of the underclasses, an incision into which the class-based managerial logic of England was to be inserted—to interdict the liberty traditions from spreading. The operant principle was Julius Caesar's "Divide and Conquer!"—a principle honed and illustrated in his immortal *Gallic Wars*. If children are divided by school class, by age-grading, by constant rankings on tests, and many other even more subtle divisions, from one another and from one's own self; the ignorant mass of mankind, divided in childhood, would never re-integrate into a dangerous whole in adulthood. As Caesar had shown, when enemy numbers are overwhelming, the strategy is to divide the enemy into factions and through the intelligent management of incentives to set these factions to battling among themselves.

8.

You needn't have studied rocket science to realize that children are easier to manipulate in this way than grownups; indeed, if children are regularly manipulated this way, it's unlikely that they can grow up. Theorists from Plato to Rousseau knew well, and explicitly taught, that if children could be kept childish beyond the natural term, if they could be cloistered in a society of children, if they could be stripped of responsibility, if their inner lives could be starved by removing the insights of historians, philosophers, economists, novelists, and religious figures, if the inevitability of suffering and death could be removed from daily consciousness and replaced with the trivializing emotions of greed, envy, jealousy, and fear—then young people would grow older but they would never grow up.

In this way a great enduring problem of supervision would be decisively minimized, for who can argue against the truth that childish and childlike people are far easier to manage than accomplished critical thinkers. With this thought in mind, you're ready to hear the six purposes of modern schooling I found in Dr. Inglis' book. The principles are his, just as he stated them nearly 100 years ago, some of the interpretive material is my own:

The first function of schooling is *adjustive*. Schools are to establish fixed habits of reaction to authority. Fixed habits. Of course this precludes critical judgement completely. If you were to devise a reliable test of whether someone had achieved fixed habits of reaction to authority, notice that requiring obedience to stupid orders would measure this better than requiring obedience to sensible orders ever could. You can't know whether someone is reflexively obedient until you can make them do foolish things.

Second is the *diagnostic* function. School is to determine each student's proper social role, logging evidence mathematically and anecdotally on cumulative records.

Third is the *sorting* function. Schools sort children by training individuals only so far as their likely destination in the social machine and not one step further. So much for making boys and girls their personal best.

The fourth function is *conformity*. As much as possible, kids are to be made alike. As egalitarian as this sounds, its purpose is to assist market and government research, people who conform are predictable.

The fifth function Inglis calls "the *hygienic* function." It has nothing to do with bodily health. It concerns what Darwin, Galton, Inglis, and many important names from the past and present would call, "the health of the race." Hygiene is a polite way of saying that school is expected to accelerate natural selection by tagging the unfit so clearly they will drop from the reproduction sweepstakes. That's what all those little humiliations from first grade onward, and all the posted lists of ranked grades are really about. The unfit will either drop out from anger, despair, or because their likely mates will accept the school's judgement of their inferiority.

And last is the *propaedutic* function. A fancy Greek term meaning that a small fraction of kids will quietly be taught how to take over management of this continuing project, made guardians of a population deliberately dumbed down and rendered childish in order that government and economic life can be managed with a minimum of hassle.

There you have it. We don't even need Karl Marx's conception of a grand warfare between classes to see that it's in the nature of complex management, economic or political, to require that most people be dumbed down, demoralized, divided from one another and from themselves, deprived of deep relationships, and discarded if they don't conform. The motives for the disgusting decisions which have to be made to bring these ends about don't have to be class-based at all, they can stem purely from greed, or fear, or self-preservation. All they require to perpetuate themselves across the years is a belief that *efficiency* is a paramount virtue, an absolute good rather than the virtue of machinery that it is.

9.

Now it's one thing to boast that you will do all those things and quite another to actually do them. What would the mechanisms to reduce people to a state where they would become compliant in such arrangements look like? Britain and Germany had both conditioned their own populations for centuries to accept paternalistic direction from the political state, but in both those countries a principal mechanism had been the state religions of Anglicanism or Lutheranism, two *Episcopal* religions which taught that the head of the political state was God's personal choice for terrestrial leadership—America had no state religion, forced schooling would have to become its stand-in.

George Orwell's post-WWII short novel called "1984" examines with uncanny precision how sophisticated the social control design of which schooling was to be a large part, really was. Simple elimination of state enemies, for instance, might be enough for tyrants like Joseph Stalin, but not for the New World order being born in the western democracies. In the new system, enemies have to be made to love their oppressors, to love their chains. Only in this elliptical fashion could the roots of opposition be poisoned. Language itself was to be corrupted by borrowing the concepts of the rebellious and redefining them so that words became unreliable as a way to know the human heart, political parties became distinctions without differences so there would be no opposition to join, privacy would be invaded to a degree where secrets were impossible.

In this new system of rational, efficient social control, allowances were made for periods of maximum public outrage. During such times, managers were instructed to retract the pseudopodia of control, and wait. Then, under cover of some national emergency like exploding office buildings, crime waves, unemployment crises, or war, the tentacles could be sent racing forward again while public attention was distracted elsewhere.

In just such a fashion the formidable common ability

to read in the U.S. was deconstructed during the drums and tramplings of World War II. A convenient and useful way to simplify what these developments added up to is to see them as ways to infantilize the general population of this nation, and then gradually through cultural outreaches to infantilize the world.

Childish people, for all the noise they make, are nearly helpless. They always fall back into line because they have no other choice, they lack the inner resources to be self-sustaining. If schooling was the principal tool, it was far from alone. Centralized popular entertainment removed the necessity to entertain oneself, easy credit removed the necessity of learning self-maintenance (until it was too late, of course), easy divorce the necessity of working at relationships, and I could go on and on—virtually every institution, including the churches, conspired to eliminate maturity in the society. And the less mature societies became, the wealthier and more stable they graze because, when management is given a free hand to work its will on a homogenized population, the road to prosperity is open. The only price that consumers have to pay is to surrender liberty, principle, morality, and mind.

10.

Toward the second half of the 19th century, beginning in the north German states of Prussia, Saxony, and Hanover, the study of scientific management was launched energetically and studied by certain prominent Americans like Horace Mann, William Torrey Harris, J.P. Morgan, Frederick Taylor, Egerton Ryerson in Canada, and by many others who envied the control the German way offered to management. They wanted that control for themselves.

A quarter century after the American civil war, a centralized corporate economy surged across the American nation. The prospect of unimaginable wealth through industrial and financial manipulations provided all the motivation powerful men of that day needed to destroy an older American—economy quite a prosperous and successful one—which made as its goal an independent livelihood for all. And which, not incidentally, demanded competence, resourcefulness, self-reliance, frugality, and stoicism from its adherents. The new corporate economy, on the other hand, demanded childishness from its employees and from its customers alike. Obviously there are more politic ways to make such a demand, to mask what was really being asked behind the rhetoric of a great advance in human affairs, but without incomplete people, without radically incomplete people, corporate culture would have been short-lived.

Oddly enough, the pioneering corporate crowd had plenty of honest (but unwitting) assistants in the great project of dumbing down the nation, and making its people less than they might have been. Utopian socialists like Robert Owen and John Ruskin thought that through an endless childhood an agrarian utopia could finally be achieved, the evolutionary crowd, including its leaders Darwin, Galton, and Herbert Spencer, thought that most of us were biologically retarded and could not grow up, scientific historians like Hegel, Herder, and Marx thought that by keeping people dumb and incomplete, history itself would finally reach a conclusion, presumably one better than present reality, and there were other forces at work which wanted a childlike public. So why have I fingered the corporations as the principal culprits who gave us our suffocating form of schooling? The answer is simple. None of the other actors who might have wished for the same denouement we got had any money; none had the resources of corporations to sustain a campaign in that direction.

So while names like the ones above, or like poor John Dewey's, are often fronted as the villains of the piece, it always required corporate financing given behind the scenes to turn an army of academic and philosophical screwballs loose to do the corporate bidding, always of course ignorant of the motives of their patrons. In Dewey's case, for instance, his reputation and influence came from his tenures at the University of Chicago and Columbia Teachers College. In both cases his principal patron was none other than John D. Rockefeller himself.

11.

I got onto the trail of a synthetically extended childhood quite by accident, through reading the last few dozen pages of an old-fashioned *History of American Education*, once quite famous, by a gentleman with the amusing name of Ellwood P. Cubberley, who at one time was a friend and correspondent of Dr. Conant at Harvard. To make Cubberley's connections with the *dramatis personae* of this talk even tighter, he was also Alexander Inglis' partner at a major American publishing house active in the textbook trade. Cubberley edited the elementary school texts, Inglis the secondary school texts. This particular publisher, Houghton Mifflin, once dominated the school trade. If you wanted a book on supervision, financing, or classroom technique back then, likely as not it would be a Houghton Mifflin book.

But Cubberley was much more than just an editor He was also Dean of Teacher Education at Stanford University, the "Harvard of the West," and head of a shadowy organization of academics nationwide who, by 1918, were in control of every major administrative post in America. If that sounds too conspiratorial to be believed, you should pick up a copy of the very conservative graduate education school text entitled *Managers of Virtue*. Its author, David Tyack, teaches at Stanford, I believe, and was once an executive in the state of Massachusetts' Department of Education. Tyack recounts the establishment of an "Education

Trust" by Cubberly and others, a kind of ultimate old boys' network to homogenize American schooling.

In 1906 Cubberly wrote that "in the new schools coming, children are to be shaped and fashioned like nails, and the specifications will come from business and government." Specifications is another way of stating particular outcomes desired, as in the recently common expression "outcomes based education." All education worth a hoot is, of course, outcomes based, the aspect which divides liberty from servitude resides in the matter of *who* decides the outcomes. A frequently used strategy in business to make workers feel that they own a piece of the action is to allow the workforce to decide a large part of how the outcomes are to be reached. This is called "management by objectives." a regime liberal about methodologies, but retaining the most conservative hold on goals.

In any event, in the last section of his frequently reprinted *History*, Cubberley *casually* mentions that childhood has been deliberately extended by four years. This is tossed off so cavalierly that it was apparent to me this was old-hat information in the circles frequented by the author, and while no details follow, from clues in the total context we can figure out how the trick was pulled off. It was done by reserving children into compounds through the advent of comprehensive confinement schooling, thus denying kids both a range of associations with the complex adult world, and a dose of responsibility. In the world of children separated from the real world, little human resources could be nurtured selectively, and held until the needs of management summoned them for application.

12.

It isn't difficult to see that the only interests served by delaying personal sovereignty are the ones of managers. Total management, whether total quality management or some other variety, and liberty are mutually contradictory terms. Once management has been professionalized, through academic degrees and other programs which establish a deep gulf between the managed and the manager, a very natural extension of managerial concern occurs in which the family and the individual come to be seen as potentially dangerous obstacles in the path of the industrial project.

Professional management minds realize that neither parents nor children can be fully trusted to see that children grow up properly, which is to say that they arrive at adulthood in a manageable state. The only sensible defense against unpleasant surprises is through centralized goal setting and frequent interventions into the maturation cycle—not to accelerate or enhance it, but just the reverse: to slow it down and retard it.

Interestingly enough, once a sound structure of schooling is built, nobody involved in maintaining it has to actually know what it was designed to do, the system will tend to grow larger and more complex, and more expensive, through a familiar bureaucratic dynamic—it will pay for political allies, and its suppliers will assist in that mightily, purely out of self-interest. Even if all the architects of the original scheme are dead, together with every knowledgeable descendant (which I'm not suggesting) the system will roll onward as a piece of autonomous social technology.

In Jonathan Messerli's biography of the early American school pioneer, Horace Mann, he quotes a diary entry Mann made after witnessing a labor parade in the Boston of the 1840's, an entry in which Mann muses that we must find a way to break the bond of association among the working classes. I'm quoting from memory but that will be close to the original. You can decide for yourself who he meant by the "we" of the statement, but the age-graded, test-ranked, Germanically ordered classroom Mann played such a large part in creating is surely a brilliant mechanism to break the bonds of association between children. And if you allow a nice seasoning of low-grade terror into the mix—and what classroom lacks that?—you have sealed the deal, for sure.

Professional management is never well served by allowing children to grow up, whatever their age, or allowing them to grow whole. Over the past several centuries, a group of higher order academic disciplines have grown up—psychology, sociology, anthropology, evolutionary biology come immediately to mind but there are more—each contending in its own way that growing up is impossible for most of us. Regardless of how many famous leftists were associated with these disciplines, all of them were underwritten by corporate or government money.

Why, you may ask? I can only speculate, of course. A pressing need of American managerial society was for some an effective substitute for the partnerships of religion and state found in Britain and Germany, our principal competitors. We were unable by constitutional law to have a state church, but state schooling wasn't so clearly proscribed. The culture could be inoculated with it by increments so that its advance to dominance would be gradual and almost invisible.

In particular, the theology of Christianity was a powerful roadblock in reaching a centralized, layered, managerial utopia. Christianity established the road to salvation as a lonely, personal struggle, whereas corporatized society was stringently *collectivized*. In corporatized society, deviants must be ostracized, goals, attitudes, feelings, and appetites must be socialized through central management of news, entertainment, schooling, and much else. Thus, Western religious thinking itself became a prime target of schooling, and Western churchmen were relentlessly bought, marginalized, or otherwise silenced.

The litany preaching that ordinary Americans and democratic processes aren't to be trusted has, by now, been preached aggressively for about 100 years. Where earlier it had been mostly a crusty relic of British colonial rule, by now it is entrenched in every corner of upperclass and upper-middle class life in America, echoing regularly through every institution of public communication, and every selective university. In the presidential election of 2000, Vice-president Gore's wife declared at a press conference that 55% of the American population was mentally disturbed and in need of therapy. And daily we hear that we must be kept under closer and closer surveillance—for our own protection. The press secretary, Ari Fleischer, said not long ago that Americans "must be careful what they say and do.' Americans of my generation would have assumed a statement like that could only be made in Imperial Japan or Nazi Germany.

13.

The profound change in the American bargain with its young wasn't the result of popular demand, nor was it caused by prominent socialists like John Dewey who are often blamed. The great transformation was an undertaking of industrial titans like Andrew Carnegie and J.P. Morgan, of John D. Rockefeller, Henry Ford, Vincent Astor, Commodore Vanderbilt, and a variety of other well thought of names from well-placed families.

If your scepticism simply won't allow this surprising assertion, I suggest you ask your librarian to secure for you two congressional reports, one made in 1915 known as the Walsh Committee Report, the other printed in 1953 as the summary of the work of the aborted Reece Commission. Both reached the same conclusion 38 years apart—American schooling has been largely the creation (and ongoing management) of a group of private corporate foundations. Just exactly why it is that no schoolteacher, school principal, or school superintendent I ever met even knows that these reports exist, I couldn't tell you—nor would I care to guess what significance this ignorance implies.

But just for the sake of argument, assume along with me that the great industrialists who owned America at the beginning of the twentieth century when institutional schooling was coming into being would not have been content to allow such a powerful shaper of young consciousness to develop in a laissez-faire way. To be fair, they couldn't afford to do that. Suppose, for instance, that universal schooling adopted the very attractive *stoic* philosophy of Roman emperor Marcus Aurelius as something to communicate vigorously to children? After all, stoic notions have served as the compass rose for huge numbers of very successful, very important people throughout history. Marcus Aurelius, the wealthiest and most powerful individual of his day, came to the conclusion, as did other stoics, that all possessions and all honors are trivial things, chains to imprison their worshippers. The truly wise, rich or poor, aim for a life in which events outside the self cannot play any part in determining the quality of time. The truly wise person should keep himself out of reach of the exterior world's power by cultivating an inner life of self-control and self-sufficiency.

The problem with encouraging this kind of thinking for everyone is that it contains the formula to utterly destroy the kind of economy that we were building around 1900 and that we find in a mature form in our world today. A high-powered commercial/industrial economy depends upon people who 1) define themselves by what they buy, and 2) become almost instantly dissatisfied with what they buy, discard it, and buy something else. It requires no great analysis to see that the two attitudes, stoicism and conspicuous consumption cannot coexist with one another. You need search no further than the *utility* of stoicism to the vast majority of lives, and the *disutility* of consumption to see why the managerial classes need to keep a close watch on bulk-process schooling. Stoicism isn't the only dangerous idea stalking outside school walls waiting to gain entry. Eternal vigilance is the price of the economy which schooling sustains.

14.

Although various notions of forced schooling had been talked about since Plato, it took unique accumulations of capital in the hands of men like Carnegie and Rockefeller, and the unique circumstances of unlimited energy which developed in the second half of the 19th century, to suggest the possibility of an industrial utopia—a place where the problem of production had been solved—was realistically at hand.

But to get there, as the most thoughtful industrialists knew, was no easy matter. Impediments of the past, like intense and wasteful competition, had to be banished and individuality, personal liberty, and conventional morality would have to be moderated if the promise of high speed machinery coupled with abundant, non-human energy was to be fulfilled. For instance, most people would have to surrender the dream of an independent livelihood if great corporations and great government agencies were to have a reliable supply of workers and executives. Or consider that mass-produced goods, as alike as pins and paperclips, require that an earlier taste for hand-crafted things be set aside. Otherwise capital investors would be reluctant to put their cash on a mass production gamble.

Put yourself in the position of these visionary industrialists, struggling to bring a new world order into being. To get the job done the majority of Americans would have to give up the independent, self-reliant values of the past and become socialized into a dependence on centralized, non-stop, intimate management. If you need an illustration of that, it's like raising your hand in school to go to the toilet.

To a very great extent the authority of the business community and the authority of the political state had to replace family tradition, religion, the wisdom of elders, or any other independent source of guidance and instruction.

It was a huge task to contemplate and there was nowhere else to start but with the children. So, drawing on methods pioneered in Prussia, the speedy arrival of young Americans at a responsible maturity had to be interdicted. Extending the period of childhood, controlling the environment of childhood, placing the children in a society of carefully selected strangers who followed orders minutely, dividing the children from one another in a variety of subtle ways, setting them into interminable, meaningless competitions so the natural bonds of sociability among them were strained to the breaking point—all these were techniques to prepare the ground for the scientific management of a vast population.

There were other agencies of socialization for mass society, too, of course. Think only of the federal income tax, which comes about in the first flush of universal forced schooling. It takes a minute's reflection to see that it isn't an instrument of revenue for the central government—the government *creates* the currency it needs—but instead a mechanism of mass surveillance, of behavioral regulation, and of intimidation. Or think of the concentration of power over the mass instruments of communication which took place early in the 20th century and has continued ever since. Through newspapers, magazines, television, radio, song, websites, and more, a relentless wave of propaganda washes over us morning to night, building and reinforcing attitudes and opinions, gushers of information we have no way to gauge the accuracy of, no way at all. The contents of our minds, in some important fashion, are built upon a foundation of faith not very different in kind from religious faith, if we depend upon media for our opinions. Think of Enron, Global Crossing, and World.com if you doubt it.

15.

If you can live with the idea that centralized masspro-duction economies must have standardized customers who are predictable to a very great degree, you are ready to consider the titanic problem men like Morgan, Carnegie, Rockefeller and the rest had undertaken—how to standardize a wildly variegated, independent-minded, libertarian-oriented domestic population. This was necessary to assure markets for the new non-stop commerce that was being anticipated, a commerce predicated on endless consumption by consumers who defined themselves by the quantity of stuff they could consume.

There were other problems, too. The biggest players in the new game had to be guaranteed some advantages over possible competition which could only be forthcoming if government itself took a discreet hand in stacking the competitive deck. The government of Britain had long been involved in just this sort of favoritism, through regulation, subsidy, virtual trust formation, and other ways. The perils of what used to be called "overproduction" and today is called "overcapacity" were clearly foreseen a century ago. In the new world order, a few would produce everything—food, news, entertainment, whatever—and the mass would consume. Similarly, a few would produce what passed for education.

Mass schooling of a compulsory nature was given its teeth in the U.S. between 1905 and 1915. Canada was often used as a testing ground to measure resistance to school changes. Bruce Cooper's *The Making of the Educational State*, demonstrates how vigorously Canadians resisted this profound incursion into the lives of families and children, to the point where police and military were frequently required to impose the new discipline.

Standardized testing, which arises after WWI, was a masterstroke of universal control, inculcating habits, fears and attitudes vital to the new regimens of comprehensive management. And the material payoff for the new management scheme came very quickly. By converting Americans into specialized economic and social functions, by foreclosing their ability to form close relationships, by reformulating personal values into public values under the watchful eye of regulators, the United States and Canada eventually achieved the most reliable domestic markets in the world. The human mutilations of schooling are a tradeoff for this prosperity—comfort and security are achieved at the price of personal sovereignty.

16.

And so we come to the paradox of extended childhood. Here in the United States we have evolved a complex, wealthy, and secure society that, at least up to a not-so-negligible point, spreads its benefits to everyone. The poor in the United States have more than the middle classes in many other societies.

Where the paradox lies is this: neither our economy nor our government can function well unless the bulk of the population is made dumb, dependent, fearful, and incomplete. We cannot encourage critical thinking because too much of that would fly in the face of our need to have most of us highly receptive to propaganda. We cannot encourage reliable morality because too many components of our economy depend upon slackness in this regard, from cigarettes, fast cars and dirty pictures to an entertainment industry centered in the glamour of murder and violence. We cannot encourage the development of principled people, because principled people are close to impossible to manage and it is the moral adaptability of our management which confers our great advantage over other nations.

Without mass forced schooling, none of the necessary qualities of a population needed to assure the continuance of this prosperous system could be guaranteed. This is what makes extending childhood through our form of schooling such a paradox, give it up and we would certainly enter a zone of great turbulence, the resolution of which nobody can predict.

17.

Once you understand the logic behind our schooling, its mechanisms and effects are fairly easy to avoid. What isn't avoidable are the tensions that come from growing up outside the mind-control machinery we've been discussing. But getting outside the box isn't hard.

Think of it this way: well-schooled people are trained to reflexively accept the opinions of their betters, to reflexively obey the commands of their superiors and to continually defer to the judgments of strangers. This is how high marks are distributed in schools. Later, when the school game is finished, the exhortations of advertisers, prominent people, and government officials will replace the orders of schoolteachers.

Well-schooled people have a low threshold of boredom. They need constant novelty to feel alive. Since they have only the flimsiest inner life—having sacrificed the time to develop one to schooling—they feel the need to constantly stay in touch with official voices through television, radio, internet, cell, commercial entertainment including music, pop journalism and shallow friendships and acquaintanceships frequently left behind for other ones.

Changing classes at short intervals is a drill to prepare kids for changing associates, domiciles, mates, and possessions in a dizzying and eternal profusion. The very air that a mass-production economy must breathe is charged with low-level dissatisfaction. If you fall in love with a pair of shoes or any other piece of stuff you buy and keep it too long, you will declare yourself a public enemy of this economy. You must be terrified into thinking that the computer you saved for a year to buy is hopelessly out of date. So too with your clothing, your home and the company you keep.

This is easy to do with those who lack an inner life. Well-schooled people require shallow training in history, philosophy, economics, literature, poetry, music, art, theology, in anything known through history to reliably develop an inner life. Well-schooled folks need life-long tutelage, not liberty, to make sense of their days. Mass journalism and mass entertainment provide that tutelage beyond schooling, to the grave.

18.

To be quit of this school nightmare demands first that we wake up to what our schools have become: they are laboratories of experimentation on young minds as well as drill centers for habits and attitudes. Schools only serve children incidentally, their principal focus is on creating the citizens that corporate business and big government managements need. I'm reluctant to be political but I see no way to avoid asking anyone in earshot to struggle for a new political awareness. Contemporary North America is neither a democracy nor a republic; it is an empire careening out of citizen control bent on projecting its own domestic control over the entire planet. Mr. Nader is right. Both major political parties work to exactly the same ends —there will be no relief from that quarter. This thing will run its course like every other empire in human history and then come crashing down from its own irrelevance to what history has shown us really matters. The best we can do politically is to hasten that day by raising our voices, by learning to say no, by arguing constantly against any and all schemes which regard ourselves and our children as "human resources."

Where the fertile field for a better tomorrow lies, it seems to me, is in a personal revolution. De-school yourself before you worry about deschooling society, fashion yourself into a fearless citizen. Make yourself into your own personal best. And do the same thing for your children and your neighbors. Extending kid's childhood is a curse on the kid's future, while a blessing of course to management. Don't allow your boy and girl to define themselves by what they consume; the prizes of such a life habit are too contemptible to be worth the cost.

And when you next find yourself appalled and disgusted by the childish and irresponsible behavior you see all around you, think of school as its forge, and do something about it.

The Lost Tools of Learning

Dorothy Leigh Sayers

THAT I, WHOSE experience of teaching is extremely limited, should presume to discuss education is a matter, surely, that calls for no apology. It is a kind of behavior to which the present climate of opinion is wholly favorable. Bishops air their opinions about economics; biologists, about metaphysics; inorganic chemists, about theology; the most irrelevant people are appointed to highly technical ministries; and plain, blunt men write to the papers to say that Epstein and Picasso do not know how to draw. Up to a certain point, and provided the criticisms are made with a reasonable modesty, these activities are commendable. Too much specialization is not a good thing. There is also one excellent reason why the veriest amateur may feel entitled to have an opinion about education. For if we are not all professional teachers, we have all, at some time or another, been taught. Even if we learnt nothing —perhaps in particular if we learnt nothing—our contribution to the discussion may have a potential value.

However, it is in the highest degree improbable that the reforms I propose will ever be carried into effect. Neither the parents, nor the training colleges, nor the examination boards, nor the boards of governors, nor the ministries of education, would countenance them for a moment. For they amount to this: that if we are to produce a society of educated people, fitted to preserve their intellectual freedom amid the complex pressures of our modern society, we must turn back the wheel of progress some four or five hundred years, to the point at which education began to lose sight of its true object, towards the end of the Middle Ages.

Before you dismiss me with the appropriate phrase—reactionary, romantic, mediaevalist, laudator temporis acti (praiser of times past), or whatever tag comes first to hand—I will ask you to consider one or two miscellaneous questions that hang about at the back, perhaps, of all our minds, and occasionally pop out to worry us.

When we think about the remarkably early age at which the young men went up to university in, let us say, Tudor times, and thereafter were held fit to assume responsibility for the conduct of their own affairs, are we altogether comfortable about that artificial prolongation of intellectual childhood and adolescence into the years of physical maturity which is so marked in our own day? To postpone the acceptance of responsibility to a late date brings with it a number of psychological complications which, while they may interest the psychiatrist, are scarcely beneficial either to the individual or to society. The stock argument in favor of postponing the school-leaving age and prolonging the period of education generally is there there is now so much more to learn than there was in the Middle Ages. This is partly true, but not wholly. The modern boy and girl are certainly taught more subjects—but does that always mean that they actually know more?

Has it ever struck you as odd, or unfortunate, that today, when the proportion of literacy throughout Western Europe is higher than it has ever been, people should have become susceptible to the influence of advertisement and mass propaganda to an extent hitherto unheard of and unimagined? Do you put this down to the mere mechanical fact that the press and the radio and so on have made propaganda much easier to distribute over a wide area? Or do you sometimes have an uneasy suspicion that the product of modern educational methods is less good than he or she might be at disentangling fact from opinion and the proven from the plausible?

Have you ever, in listening to a debate among adult and presumably responsible people, been fretted by the extraordinary inability of the average debater to speak to the question, or to meet and refute the arguments of speakers on the other side? Or have you ever pondered upon the extremely high incidence of irrelevant matter which crops up at committee meetings, and upon the very great rarity of persons capable of acting as chairmen of committees? And when you think of this, and think that most of our public affairs are settled by debates and committees, have you ever felt a certain sinking of the heart?

Have you ever followed a discussion in the newspapers or elsewhere and noticed how frequently writers fail to define the terms they use? Or how often, if one man does define his terms, another will assume in his reply that he was using the terms in precisely the opposite sense to that in which he has already defined them? Have you ever been faintly troubled by the amount of slipshod syntax going about? And, if so, are you troubled because it is inelegant or because it may lead to dangerous misunderstanding?

Do you ever find that young people, when they have left school, not only forget most of what they have learnt (that is only to be expected), but forget also, or betray that they have never really known, how to tackle a new subject for themselves? Are you often bothered by coming across grown-up men and women who seem unable to distinguish between a book that is sound, scholarly, and properly documented, and one that is, to any trained eye, very conspicuously none of these things? Or who cannot handle a library catalogue? Or who, when faced with a book of reference, betray a curious inability to extract from it the passages relevant to the particular question which interests them?

Do you often come across people for whom, all their lives, a "subject" remains a "subject," divided by watertight bulkheads from all other "subjects," so that they experience very great difficulty in making an immediate mental connection between let us say, algebra and detective fiction, sewage disposal and the price of salmon—or, more generally, between such spheres of knowledge as philosophy and economics, or chemistry and art?

Are you occasionally perturbed by the things written by adult men and women for adult men and women to read? We find a well-known biologist writing in a weekly paper to the effect that: "It is an argument against the existence of a Creator (I think he put it more strongly; but since I have, most unfortunately, mislaid the reference, I will put his claim at its lowest)—"an argument against the existence of a Creator that the same kind of variations which are produced by natural selection can be produced at will by stock breeders." One might feel tempted to say that it is rather an argument for the existence of a Creator. Actually, of course, it is neither; all it proves is that the same material causes (recombination of the chromosomes, by crossbreeding, and so forth) are sufficient to account for all observed variations just as the various combinations of the same dozen tones are materially sufficient to account for Beethoven's *Moonlight Sonata* and the noise the cat makes by walking on the keys. But the cat's performance neither proves nor disproves the existence of Beethoven; and all that is proved by the biologist's argument is that he was unable to distinguish between a material and a final cause.

Here is a sentence from no less academic a source than a front-page article in the Times Literary Supplement: "The Frenchman, Alfred Epinas, pointed out that certain species (e.g., ants and wasps) can only face the horrors of life and death in association." I do not know what the Frenchman actually did say; what the Englishman says he said is patently meaningless. We cannot know whether life holds any horror for the ant, nor in what sense the isolated wasp which you kill upon the windowpane can be said to "face" or not to "face" the horrors of death. The subject of the article is mass behavior in man; and the human motives have been unobtrusively transferred from the main proposition to the supporting instance. Thus the argument, in effect, assumes what it set out to prove—a fact which would become immediately apparent if it were presented in a formal syllogism. This is only a small and haphazard example of a vice which pervades whole books—particularly books written by men of science on metaphysical subjects.

Another quotation from the same issue of the TLS comes in fittingly here to wind up this random collection of disquieting thoughts—this time from a review of Sir Richard Livingstone's "Some Tasks for Education": "More than once the reader is reminded of the value of an intensive study of at least one subject, so as to learn 'the meaning of knowledge' and what precision and persistence is needed to attain it. Yet there is elsewhere full recognition of the distressing fact that a man may be master in one field and show no better judgment than his neighbor anywhere else; he remembers what he has learnt, but forgets altogether how he learned it."

I would draw your attention particularly to that last sentence, which offers an explanation of what the writer rightly calls the "distressing fact" that the intellectual skills bestowed upon us by our education are not readily transferable to subjects other than those in which we acquired them: "he remembers what he has learnt, but forgets altogether how he learned it."

Is not the great defect of our education today—a defect traceable through all the disquieting symptoms of trouble that I have mentioned—that although we often succeed in teaching our pupils "subjects," we fail lamentably on the whole in teaching them how to think: they learn everything, except the art of learning. It is as though we had taught a child, mechanically and by rule of thumb, to play "The Harmonious Blacksmith" upon the piano, but had never taught him the scale or how to read music; so that, having memorized "The Harmonious Blacksmith," he still had not the faintest notion how to proceed from that to tackle "The Last Rose of Summer." Why do I say, "as though?" In certain of the arts and crafts, we sometimes do precisely this—requiring a child to "express himself" in paint before we teach him how to handle the colors and the brush. There is a school of thought which believes this to be the right way to set about the job. But observe: it is not the way in which a trained craftsman will go about to teach himself a new medium. He, having learned by experience the best way to economize labor and take the thing by the right end, will start off by doodling about on an odd piece of material, in order to give himself the feel of the tool.

Let us now look at the mediaeval scheme of education —the syllabus of the Schools. It does not matter, for the moment, whether it was devised for small children or for older students, or how long people were supposed to take over it. What matters is the light it throws upon what the men of the Middle Ages supposed to be the object and the right order of the educative process.

The syllabus was divided into two parts: the Trivium and Quadrivium. The second part—the Quadrivium—consisted of "subjects," and need not for the moment concern us. The interesting thing for us is the composition of the Trivium, which preceded the Quadrivium and was the preliminary discipline for it. It consisted of three parts: Grammar, Dialectic, and Rhetoric, in that order.

Now the first thing we notice is that two at any rate of these "subjects" are not what we should call subjects" at all: they are only methods of dealing with subjects. Grammar, indeed, is a "subject" in the sense that it does mean definitely learning a language—at that period it meant learning Latin. But language itself is simply the medium in which thought is expressed. The whole of the Trivium was, in fact, intended to teach the pupil the proper use of the tools of learning, before he began to apply them to subjects" at all. First, he learned a language; not just how to order a meal in a foreign language, but the structure of a language, and hence of language itself—what it was, how it was put together, and how it worked. Secondly, he learned how to use language; how to define his terms and make accurate statements; how to construct an argument and how to detect fallacies in argument. Dialectic, that is to say, embraced Logic and Disputation. Thirdly, he learned to express himself in language—how to say what he had to say elegantly and persuasively.

At the end of his course, he was required to compose a thesis upon some theme set by his masters or chosen by himself, and afterwards to defend his thesis against the criticism of the faculty. By this time, he would have learned—or woe betide him—not merely to write an essay on paper, but to speak audibly and intelligibly from a platform, and to use his wits quickly when heckled. There would also be questions, cogent and shrewd, from those who had already run the gauntlet of debate.

It is, of course, quite true that bits and pieces of the mediaeval tradition still linger, or have been revived, in the ordinary school syllabus of today. Some knowledge of grammar is still required when learning a foreign language—perhaps I should say, is again required," for during my own lifetime, we passed through a phase when the teaching of declensions and conjugations was considered rather reprehensible, and it was considered better to pick these things up as we went along. School debating societies flourish; essays are written; the necessity for "self-expression" is stressed, and perhaps even over-stressed. But these activities are cultivated more or less in detachment, as belonging to the special subjects in which they are pigeon-holed rather than as forming one coherent scheme of mental training to which all "subjects" stand in a subordinate relation. "Grammar" belongs especially to the "subject" of foreign languages, and essay-writing to the "subject" called "English"; while Dialectic has become almost entirely divorced from the rest of the curriculum, and is frequently practiced unsystematically and out of school hours as a separate exercise, only very loosely related to the main business of learning. Taken by and large, the great difference of emphasis between the two conceptions holds good: modern education concentrates on "teaching subjects," leaving the method of thinking, arguing, and expressing one's conclusions to be picked up by the scholar as he goes along. Mediaeval education concentrated on first forging and learning to handle the tools of learning, using whatever subject came handy as a piece of material on which to doodle until the use of the tool became second nature.

"Subjects" of some kind there must be, of course. One cannot learn the theory of grammar without learning an actual language, or learn to argue and orate without speaking about something in particular. The debating subjects of the Middle Ages were drawn largely from theology, or from the ethics and history of antiquity. Often, indeed, they became stereotyped, especially towards the end of the period, and the far-fetched and wire-drawn absurdities of Scholastic argument fretted Milton and provide food for merriment even to this day. Whether they were in themselves any more hackneyed and trivial then the usual subjects set nowadays for "essay writing" I should not like to say: we may ourselves grow a little weary of "A Day in My Holidays" and all the rest of it. But most of the merriment is misplaced, because the aim and object of the debating thesis has by now been lost sight of.

A glib speaker in the Brains Trust once entertained his audience (and reduced the late Charles Williams to helpless rage) by asserting that in the Middle Ages it was a matter of faith to know how many archangels could dance on the point of a needle. I need not say, I hope, that it never was a "matter of faith"; it was simply a debating exercise, whose set subject was the nature of angelic substance: were angels material, and if so, did they occupy space? The answer usually adjudged correct is, I believe, that angels are pure intelligences; not material, but limited, so that they may have location in space but not extension. An analogy might be drawn from human thought, which is similarly non-material and similarly limited. Thus, if your thought is concentrated upon one thing—say, the point of a needle—it is located there in the sense that it is not elsewhere; but although it is "there," it occupies no space there, and there is nothing to prevent an infinite number of different people's thoughts being concentrated upon the same needle-point at the same time. The proper subject of the argument is thus seen to be the distinction between location and extension in space; the matter on which the argument is exercised happens to be the nature of angels (although, as we have seen, it might equally well have been something else); the practical lesson to be drawn from the argument is not to use words like "there" in a loose and unscientific way, without specifying whether you mean "located there" or "occupying space there."

Scorn in plenty has been poured out upon the mediaeval passion for hair-splitting; but when we look at the shameless abuse made, in print and on the platform, of controversial expressions with shifting and ambiguous connotations, we may feel it in our hearts to wish that every reader and hearer had been so defensively armored by his education as to be able to cry: "Distinguo."

For we let our young men and women go out unarmed, in a day when armor was never so necessary. By teaching them all to read, we have left them at the mercy of the printed word. By the invention of the film and the radio, we have made certain that no aversion to reading shall secure them from the incessant battery of words, words, words. They do not know what the words mean; they do not know how toward them off or blunt their edge or fling them back; they are a prey to words in their emotions instead of being the masters of them in their intellects. We who were scandalized in 1940 when men were sent to fight armored tanks with rifles, are not scandalized when young men and women are sent into the world to fight massed propaganda with a smattering of "subjects"; and when whole classes and whole nations become hypnotized by the arts of the spell binder, we have the impudence to be astonished. We dole out lip-service to the importance of education—lip-service and, just occasionally, a little grant of money; we postpone the school-leaving age, and plan to build bigger and better schools; the teachers slave conscientiously in and out of school hours; and yet, as I believe, all this devoted effort is largely frustrated, because we have lost the tools of learning, and in their absence can only make a botched and piecemeal job of it.

What, then, are we to do? We cannot go back to the Middle Ages. That is a cry to which we have become accustomed. We cannot go back—or can we? "Distinguo." I should like every term in that proposition defined. Does go back mean a retrogression in time, or the revision of an error? The first is clearly impossible per se; the second is a thing which wise men do every day. "Cannot"—does this mean that our behavior is determined irreversibly, or merely that such an action would be very difficult in view of the opposition it would provoke? Obviously the twentieth century is not and cannot be the fourteenth; but if "the Middle Ages" is, in this context, simply a picturesque phrase denoting a particular educational theory, there seems to be no a priori reason why we should not "go back" to it—with modifications—as we have already "gone back" with modifications, to, let us say, the idea of playing Shakespeare's plays as he wrote them, and not in the "modernized" versions of Cibber and Garrick, which once seemed to be the latest thing in theatrical progress

Let us amuse ourselves by imagining that such progressive retrogression is possible. Let us make a clean sweep of all educational authorities, and furnish ourselves with a nice little school of boys and girls whom we may experimentally equip for the intellectual conflict along lines chosen by ourselves. We will endow them with exceptionally docile parents; we will staff our school with teachers who are themselves perfectly familiar with the aims and methods of the Trivium; we will have our building and staff large enough to allow our classes to be small enough for adequate handling; and we will postulate a Board of Examiners willing and qualified to test the products we turn out. Thus prepared, we will attempt to sketch out a syllabus—a modern Trivium "with modifications" and we will see where we get to.

But first: what age shall the children be? Well, if one is to educate them on novel lines, it will be better that they should have nothing to unlearn; besides, one cannot begin a good thing too early, and the Trivium is by its nature not learning, but a preparation for learning. We will, therefore, "catch 'em young," requiring of our pupils only that they shall be able to read, write, and cipher.

My views about child psychology are, I admit, neither orthodox nor enlightened. Looking back upon myself (since I am the child I know best and the only child I can pretend to know from inside) I recognize three states of development. These, in a rough-and-ready fashion, I will call the Poll-Parrot, the Pert, and the Poetic—the latter coinciding, approximately, with the onset of puberty. The Poll-Parrot stage is the one in which learning by heart is easy and, on the whole, pleasurable; whereas reasoning is difficult and, on the whole, little relished. At this age, one readily memorizes the shapes and appearances of things; one likes to recite the number-plates of cars; one rejoices in the chanting of rhymes and the rumble and thunder of unintelligible polysyllables; one enjoys the mere accumulation of things. The Pert age, which follows upon this (and, naturally, overlaps it to some extent), is characterized by contradicting, answering back, liking to "catch people out" (especially one's elders); and by the propounding of conundrums. Its nuisance-value is extremely high. It usually sets in about the Fourth Form. The Poetic age is popularly known as the "difficult" age. It is self-centered; it yearns to express itself; it rather specializes in being misunderstood; it is restless and tries to achieve independence; and, with good luck and good guidance, it should show the beginnings of creativeness; a reaching out towards a synthesis of what it already knows, and a deliberate eagerness to know and do some one thing in preference to all others. Now it seems to me that the layout of the Trivium adapts itself with a singular appropriateness to these three ages: Grammar to the Poll-Parrot, Dialectic to the Pert, and Rhetoric to the Poetic age.

Let us begin, then, with Grammar. This, in practice, means the grammar of some language in particular; and it must be an inflected language. The grammatical structure of an uninflected language is far too analytical to be tackled by any one without previous practice in Dialectic. Moreover, the inflected languages interpret the uninflected, whereas the uninflected are of little use in interpreting the inflected. I will say at once, quite firmly, that the best grounding for education is the Latin grammar. I say this, not because Latin is traditional and mediaeval, but simply because even a rudimentary knowledge of Latin cuts down the labor and pains of learning almost any other subject by at least fifty percent. It is the key to the vocabulary and structure of all the Romance languages and the structure of all the Teutonic languages, as well as to the technical vocabulary of all the sciences and to the literature of the entire Mediterranean civilization, together with all its historical documents.

Those whose pedantic preference for a living language persuades them to deprive their pupils of all these advantages might substitute Russian, whose grammar is still more primitive. Russian is, of course, helpful with the other Slav dialects. There is something also to be said for Classical Greek. But my own choice is Latin. Having thus pleased the Classicists among you, I will proceed to horrify them by adding that I do not think it either wise or necessary to cramp the ordinary pupil upon the Procrustean bed of the Augustan Age, with its highly elaborate and artificial verse forms and oratory. Post-classical and mediaeval Latin, which was a living language right down to the end of the Renaissance, is easier and in some ways livelier; a study of it helps to dispel the widespread notion that learning and literature came to a full stop when Christ was born and only woke up again at the Dissolution of the Monasteries.

Latin should be begun as early as possible—at a time when inflected speech seems no more astonishing than any other phenomenon in an astonishing world; and when the chanting of "Amo, amas, amat" is as ritually agreeable to the feelings as the chanting of "eeny, meeny, miney, moe."

During this age we must, of course, exercise the mind on other things besides Latin grammar. Observation and memory are the faculties most lively at this period; and if we are to learn a contemporary foreign language we should begin now, before the facial and mental muscles become rebellious to strange intonations. Spoken French or German can be practiced alongside the grammatical discipline of the Latin.

In English, meanwhile, verse and prose can be learned by heart, and the pupil's memory should be stored with stories of every kind—classical myth, European legend, and so forth. I do not think that the classical stories and masterpieces of ancient literature should be made the vile bodies on which to practice the techniques of Grammar—that was a fault of mediaeval education which we need not perpetuate. The stories can be enjoyed and remembered in English, and related to their origin at a subsequent stage. Recitation aloud should be practiced, individually or in chorus; for we must not forget that we are laying the groundwork for Disputation and Rhetoric.

The grammar of History should consist, I think, of dates, events, anecdotes, and personalities. A set of dates to which one can peg all later historical knowledge is of enormous help later on in establishing the perspective of history. It does not greatly matter which dates: those of the Kings of England will do very nicely, provided that they are accompanied by pictures of costumes, architecture, and other everyday things, so that the mere mention of a date calls up a very strong visual presentment of the whole period.

Geography will similarly be presented in its factual aspect, with maps, natural features, and visual presentment of customs, costumes, flora, fauna, and so on; and I believe myself that the discredited and old-fashioned memorizing of a few capitol cities, rivers, mountain ranges, etc., does no harm. Stamp collecting may be encouraged.

Science, in the Poll-Parrot period, arranges itself naturally and easily around collections—the identifying and naming of specimens and, in general, the kind of thing that used to be called "natural philosophy." To know the name and properties of things is, at this age, a satisfaction in itself; to recognize a devil's coach-horse at sight, and assure one's foolish elders, that, in spite of its appearance, it does not sting; to be able to pick out Cassiopeia and the Pleiades and perhaps even to know who Cassiopeia and the Pleiades were; to be aware that a whale is not a fish, and a bat not a bird—all these things give a pleasant sensation of superiority; while to know a ring snake from an adder or a poisonous from an edible toadstool is a kind of knowledge that also has practical value.

The grammar of Mathematics begins, of course, with the multiplication table, which, if not learnt now, will never be learnt with pleasure; and with the recognition of geometrical shapes and the grouping of numbers. These exercises lead naturally to the doing of simple sums in arithmetic. More complicated mathematical processes may, and perhaps should, be postponed, for the reasons which will presently appear.

So far (except, of course, for the Latin), our curriculum contains nothing that departs very far from common practice.

The difference will be felt rather in the attitude of the teachers, who must look upon all these activities less as "subjects" in themselves than as a gathering-together of material for use in the next part of the Trivium. What that material is, is only of secondary importance; but it is as well that anything and everything which can be usefully committed to memory should be memorized at this period, whether it is immediately intelligible or not. The modern tendency is to try and force rational explanations on a child's mind at too early an age. Intelligent questions, spontaneously asked, should, of course, receive an immediate and rational answer; but it is a great mistake to suppose that a child cannot readily enjoy and remember things that are beyond his power to analyze—particularly if those things have a strong imaginative appeal (as, for example, "Kubla Kahn"), an attractive jingle (like some of the memory-rhymes for Latin genders), or an abundance of rich, resounding polysyllables (like the Quicunque Vult).

This reminds me of the grammar of Theology. I shall add it to the curriculum, because theology is the mistress-science without which the whole educational structure will necessarily lack its final synthesis. Those who disagree about this will remain content to leave their pupil's education still full of loose ends. This will matter rather less than it might, since by the time that the tools of learning have been forged the student will be able to tackle theology for himself, and will probably insist upon doing so and making sense of it. Still, it is as well to have this matter also handy and ready for the reason to work upon. At the grammatical age, therefore, we should become acquainted with the story of God and Man in outline—i.e., the Old and New Testaments presented as parts of a single narrative of Creation, Rebellion, and Redemption—and also with the Creed, the Lord's Prayer, and the Ten Commandments. At this early stage, it does not matter nearly so much that these things should be fully understood as that they should be known and remembered.

It is difficult to say at what age, precisely, we should pass from the first to the second part of the Trivium. Generally speaking, the answer is: so soon as the pupil shows himself disposed to pertness and interminable argument. For as, in the first part, the master faculties are Observation and Memory, so, in the second, the master faculty is the Discursive Reason. In the first, the exercise to which the rest of the material was, as it were, keyed, was the Latin grammar; in the second, the key-exercise will be Formal Logic. It is here that our curriculum shows its first sharp divergence from modern standards. The disrepute into which Formal Logic has fallen is entirely unjustified; and its neglect is the root cause of nearly all those disquieting symptoms which we have noted in the modern intellectual constitution. Logic has been discredited, partly because we have come to suppose that we are conditioned almost entirely by the intuitive and the unconscious. There is no time to argue whether this is true; I will simply observe that to neglect the proper training of the reason is the best possible way to make it true. Another cause for the disfavor into which Logic has fallen is the belief that it is entirely based upon universal assumptions that are either unprovable or tautological. This is not true. Not all universal propositions are of this kind. But even if they were, it would make no difference, since every syllogism whose major premise is in the form "All A is B" can be recast in hypothetical form. Logic is the art of arguing correctly: "If A, then B." The method is not invalidated by the hypothetical character of A. Indeed, the practical utility of Formal Logic today lies not so much in the establishment of positive conclusions as in the prompt detection and exposure of invalid inference.

Let us now quickly review our material and see how it is to be related to Dialectic. On the Language side, we shall now have our vocabulary and morphology at our fingertips; henceforward we can concentrate on syntax and analysis (i.e., the logical construction of speech) and the history of language (i.e., how we came to arrange our speech as we do in order to convey our thoughts).

Our Reading will proceed from narrative and lyric to essays, argument and criticism, and the pupil will learn to try his own hand at writing this kind of thing. Many lessons—on whatever subject—will take the form of debates; and the place of individual or choral recitation will be taken by dramatic performances, with special attention to plays in which an argument is stated in dramatic form.

Mathematics—algebra, geometry, and the more advanced

kinds of arithmetic—will now enter into the syllabus and take its place as what it really is: not a separate subject but a sub-department of Logic. It is neither more nor less than the rule of the syllogism in its particular application to number and measurement, and should be taught as such, instead of being, for some, a dark mystery, and, for others, a special revelation, neither illuminating nor illuminated by any other part of knowledge.

History, aided by a simple system of ethics derived from the grammar of theology, will provide much suitable material for discussion: Was the behavior of this statesman justified? What was the effect of such an enactment? What are the arguments for and against this or that form of government? We shall thus get an introduction to constitutional history—a subject meaningless to the young child, but of absorbing interest to those who are prepared to argue and debate. Theology itself will furnish material for argument about conduct and morals; and should have its scope extended by a simplified course of dogmatic theology (i.e., the rational structure of Christian thought), clarifying the relations between the dogma and the ethics, and lending itself to that application of ethical principles in particular instances which is properly called casuistry. ences will likewise provide material for Dialectic.

But above all, we must not neglect the material which is so abundant in the pupils' own daily life. There is a delightful passage in Leslie Paul's "The Living Hedge" which tells how a number of small boys enjoyed themselves for days arguing about an extraordinary shower of rain which had fallen in their town—a shower so localized that it left one half of the main street wet and the other dry. Could one, they argued, properly say that it had rained that day on or over the town or only in the town? How many drops of water were required to constitute rain? And so on. Argument about this led on to a host of similar problems about rest and motion, sleep and waking, "est and non est," and the infinitesimal division of time. The whole passage is an admirable example of the spontaneous development of the ratiocinative faculty and the natural and proper thirst of the awakening reason for the definition of terms and exactness of statement. All events are food for such an appetite.

An umpire's decision; the degree to which one may transgress the spirit of a regulation without being trapped by the letter: on such questions as these, children are born casuists, and their natural propensity only needs to be developed and trained—and especially, brought into an intelligible relationship with the events in the grown-up world. The newspapers are full of good material for such exercises: legal decisions, on the one hand, in cases where the cause at issue is not too abstruse; on the other, fallacious reasoning and muddleheaded arguments, with which the correspondence columns of certain papers one could name are abundantly stocked.

Wherever the matter for Dialectic is found, it is, of course, highly important that attention should be focused upon the beauty and economy of a fine demonstration or a well-turned argument, lest veneration should wholly die. Criticism must not be merely destructive; though at the same time both teacher and pupils must be ready to detect fallacy, slipshod reasoning, ambiguity, irrelevance, and redundancy, and to pounce upon them like rats. This is the moment when precis-writing may be usefully undertaken; together with such exercises as the writing of an essay, and the reduction of it, when written, by 25 or 50 percent.

It will, doubtless, be objected that to encourage young persons at the Pert age to browbeat, correct, and argue with their elders will render them perfectly intolerable. My answer is that children of that age are intolerable anyhow; and that their natural argumentativeness may just as well be canalized to good purpose as allowed to run away into the sands. It may, indeed, be rather less obtrusive at home if it is disciplined in school; and anyhow, elders who have abandoned the wholesome principle that children should be seen and not heard have no one to blame but themselves.

Once again, the contents of the syllabus at this stage may be anything you like. The "subjects" supply material; but they are all to be regarded as mere grist for the mental mill to work upon. The pupils should be encouraged to go and forage for their own information, and so guided towards the proper use of libraries and books for reference, and shown how to tell which sources are authoritative and which are not.

Towards the close of this stage, the pupils will probably

be beginning to discover for themselves that their knowledge and experience are insufficient, and that their trained intelligences need a great deal more material to chew upon. The imagination—usually dormant during the Pert age—will reawaken, and prompt them to suspect the limitations of logic and reason. This means that they are passing into the Poetic age and are ready to embark on the study of Rhetoric. The doors of the storehouse of knowledge should now be thrown open for them to browse about as they will. The things once learned by rote will be seen in new contexts; the things once coldly analyzed can now be brought together to form a new synthesis; here and there a sudden insight will bring about that most exciting of all discoveries: the realization that truism is true.

It is difficult to map out any general syllabus for the study of Rhetoric: a certain freedom is demanded. In literature, appreciation should be again allowed to take the lead over destructive criticism; and self-expression in writing can go forward, with its tools now sharpened to cut clean and observe proportion. Any child who already shows a disposition to specialize should be given his head: for, when the use of the tools has been well and truly learned, it is available for any study whatever. It would be well, I think, that each pupil should learn to do one, or two, subjects really well, while taking a few classes in subsidiary subjects so as to keep his mind open to the inter-relations of all knowledge. Indeed, at this stage, our difficulty will be to keep "subjects" apart;

for Dialectic will have shown all branches of learning to be inter-related, so Rhetoric will tend to show that all knowledge is one. To show this, and show why it is so, is pre-eminently the task of the mistress science. But whether theology is studied or not, we should at least insist that children who seem inclined to specialize on the mathematical and scientific side should be obliged to attend some lessons in the humanities and vice versa. At this stage, also, the Latin grammar, having done its work, may be dropped for those who prefer to carry on their language studies on the modern side; while those who are likely never to have any great use or aptitude for mathematics might also be allowed to rest, more or less, upon their oars. Generally speaking, whatsoever is mere apparatus may now be allowed to fall into the background, while the trained mind is gradually prepared for specialization in the "subjects" which, when the Trivium is completed, it should be perfectly well equipped to tackle on its own. The final synthesis of the Trivium—the presentation and public defense of the thesis—should be restored in some form; perhaps as a kind of "leaving examination" during the last term at school.

The scope of Rhetoric depends also on whether the pupil is to be turned out into the world at the age of sixteen or whether he is to proceed to the university. Since, really, Rhetoric should be taken at about fourteen, the first category of pupil should study Grammar from about nine to eleven, and Dialectic from twelve to fourteen; his last two school years would then be devoted to

Rhetoric, which, in this case, would be of a fairly specialized and vocational kind, suiting him to enter immediately upon some practical career. A pupil of the second category would finish his Dialectical course in his preparatory school, and take Rhetoric during his first two years at his public school. At sixteen, he would be ready to start upon those "subjects" which are proposed for his later study at the university: and this part of his education will correspond to the mediaeval Quadrivium. What this amounts to is that the ordinary pupil, whose formal education ends at sixteen, will take the Trivium only; whereas scholars will take both the Trivium and the Quadrivium.

Is the Trivium, then, a sufficient education for life? Properly taught, I believe that it should be. At the end of the Dialectic, the children will probably seem to be far behind their coevals brought up on old-fashioned "modern" methods, so far as detailed knowledge of specific subjects is concerned. But after the age of fourteen they should be able to overhaul the others hand over fist. Indeed, I am not at all sure that a pupil thoroughly proficient in the Trivium would not be fit to proceed immediately to the university at the age of sixteen, thus proving himself the equal of his mediaeval counterpart, whose precocity astonished us at the beginning of this discussion. This, to be sure, would make hay of the English public-school system, and disconcert the universities very much. It would, for example, make quite a different thing of the Oxford and Cambridge boat race.

But I am not here to consider the feelings of academic bodies: I am concerned only with the proper training of the mind to encounter and deal with the formidable mass of undigested problems presented to it by the modern world. For the tools of learning are the same, in any and every subject; and the person who knows how to use them will, at any age, get the mastery of a new subject in half the time and with a quarter of the effort expended by the person who has not the tools at his command. To learn six subjects without remembering how they were learnt does nothing to ease the approach to a seventh; to have learnt and remembered the art of learning makes the approach to every subject an open door.

Before concluding these necessarily very sketchy suggestions, I ought to say why I think it necessary, in these days, to go back to a discipline which we had discarded. The truth is that for the last three hundred years or so we have been living upon our educational capital. The post-Renaissance world, bewildered and excited by the profusion of new "subjects" offered to it, broke away from the old discipline (which had, indeed, become sadly dull and stereotyped in its practical application) and imagined that henceforward it could, as it were, disport itself happily in its new and extended Quadrivium without passing through the Trivium. But the Scholastic tradition, though broken and maimed, still lingered in the public schools and universities: Milton, however much he protested against it, was formed by it—the debate of the

Fallen Angels and the disputation of Abdiel with Satan have the toolmarks of the Schools upon them, and might, incidentally, profitably figure as set passages for our Dialectical studies. Right down to the nineteenth century, our public affairs were mostly managed, and our books and journals were for the most part written, by people brought up in homes, and trained in places, where that tradition was still alive in the memory and almost in the blood. Just so, many people today who are atheist or agnostic in religion, are governed in their conduct by a code of Christian ethics which is so rooted that it never occurs to them to question it.

But one cannot live on capital forever. However firmly a tradition is rooted, if it is never watered, though it dies hard, yet in the end it dies. And today a great number — perhaps the majority —of the men and women who handle our affairs, write our books and our newspapers, carry out our research, present our plays and our films, speak from our platforms and pulpits—yes, and who educate our young people—have never, even in a lingering traditional memory, undergone the Scholastic discipline. Less and less do the children who come to be educated bring any of that tradition with them. We have lost the tools of learning—the axe and the wedge, the hammer and the saw, the chisel and the plane—that were so adaptable to all tasks. Instead of them, we have merely a set of complicated jigs, each of which will do but one task and no more, and in using which eye and hand receive no training, so that no man ever sees the work as a whole or "looks to the end of the work."

What use is it to pile task on task and prolong the days of labor, if at the close the chief object is left unattained? It is not the fault of the teachers—they work only too hard already. The combined folly of a civilization that has forgotten its own roots is forcing them to shore up the tottering weight of an educational structure that is built upon sand. They are doing for their pupils the work which the pupils themselves ought to do. For the sole true end of education is simply this: to teach men how to learn for themselves; and whatever instruction fails to do this is effort spent in vain.

Is a *Head* Start Damaging Our Children's *Hearts*?

Elizabeth Y. Hanson

"Give me a child until he is seven and I will show you the man."

ARISTOTLE

IS IT POSSIBLE that, with the best of intentions as loving parents, we are hurting our children's emotional development by thrusting upon them formal academic learning during their early years, otherwise known as school?

In spite of modern research findings, most children are in first grade in a public or private school by the age of six, having first spent a couple of years in preschool programs designed to prepare them for first grade. Is it possible that pushing our children into academics—language, arts, and mathematics—at such an early age may not be a practice that's beneficial to children?

Western child-development psychologists have long understood that requiring children to perform academically at too early an age interferes with their emotional development, but this finding has been largely ignored to the detriment of our children.

Prior to the 1960s, preschools were considered institutions where unfortunate children were placed, and society looked upon the families of these children with pity. Either the children had lost their fathers to death or divorce, or he did not earn enough to provide for his family, so their mother worked to supplement his income.

Keep in mind that mothers preferred to stay home and tend to their children, because society placed importance upon the mother's role as an irreplaceable primary caregiver. Supplementing the family income to buy a larger home, an extra car, or take fancier vacations was not a part of the pre-1970s mindset. Working mothers were simply doing what was required of them to help keep their families off the streets.

It wasn't until the 1970s that this attitude toward the needs of children began to change. With President Johnson's marketing campaign to give children a "head start", over a matter of a few years, preschools became popular places for children. The 1970s belief that if children had an early start with academic subjects, they would be smarter and perform better academically, had quickly swept into every American home. After all, what loving mother would not want her child to be smarter and excel in academics, paving the road for a greater chance at "success"?

However, in traditional thought the emphasis was not on a *head* start, but a *heart* start. The heart was known to be the seat of the emotions and one was counseled to control one's emotions or passions to improve one's character. The state of the heart was considered of graver importance than the strength of the intellect, because living a "good" life was, and still is, predicated upon having a good character.

It wasn't that we disregarded the training of the mind, but only that character development was not abandoned in the name of education. Children, when young, needed their mothers and the safety of their homes to nurture their hearts, they did *not* need school.

Are we, then, damaging the ability of our children to develop a sound emotional foundation—and therefore a sound heart—by pushing them into formal academic learning too early?

In our well-intended efforts to provide our children with a *head* start, are we neglecting to provide them with a *heart* start?

The Benefits of Play

It has been conventional wisdom that play is the work of young children. During the first five years of life, a child lives—and plays—in a world where the real and the imaginary are united. Between the ages of five and seven this unification begins to split and the child gradually departs from his unique world, and begins to enter what is known as the "age of reason." Around age seven, this split is complete and the child is now able to distinguish the real from the imaginary. Now, having entered the age of discernment, the child can determine right from wrong and is capable of moral responsibility.

Those early years are crucial for laying a strong emotional foundation that will serve our children well throughout their lives. And unstructured play is one of the means through which children build such a foundation; other means include, of course, a safe and nurturing home environment, healthy adult role models, and the absence of childhood trauma. It is through this time spent in play that children develop a host of skills that are essential for a successful life: creativity and imagination, resilience, empathy, the ability to work and get along with others, the art of negotiation, as well as self-control and self-discipline.

Take, for instance, the make-believe games children play.

A child can literally turn a stick into a spirited horse, a box into a glorious castle, or a beat-up rag doll into a royal princess. If you tell the child, "No, that's a stick, not a horse!", you may have an angry or confused child on your hands. That stick is as much a horse to the child as a real horse is to an adult. It is largely through such make-believe games that children develop their imagination and creative processes. People with limited imaginations tend to think in more concrete, black and white terms. Original thoughts and novel ideas require the ability to think in the abstract at greater degrees and are dependent upon a strong imagination and sense of creativity.

Games played in childhood also help children develop their ability to empathize with others. In order to understand how another person feels or have compassion for that person, we must first learn to walk in their shoes. That is exactly what a little girl is doing when she pretends to be a mother, a doctor, or even a queen. It is what a little boy does when he pretends to be a father, a knight, or a fireman. They are assuming the identity of another human being, imagining what it is like to think, feel, and be that person. Playing these games over and over again develops the child's ability to feel and identify with another person's experience, eventually helping them grow into an empathetic adult.

Empathy, or the ability to experience another's feelings, is a virtue that is angelic in nature. The more empathy one possesses, the more one is able to embody the ideal qualities of mercy, compassion and an unconditional love for others. On the contrary, the absence of empathy renders a person capable of committing the most heinous acts against another human being, crimes that are considered demonic. It is worth noting that studies on serial killers show that play time was often absent from their childhood experience. While play time isn't necessarily absent from the lives of schoolchildren, it can't be ignored that children who are put into early education programs have less time for unstructured play—the kind of play that matters most—than children who remain safely in the care of their families.

Learning to play with other children of varying ages is essential to developing strong social skills. By the age of four, children begin to make up goal-driven games that they can play together, such as pretending to be pirates who are hunting for a treasure chest. They decide what kind of a game to play, they determine how the game will be played, and they decide the role of each player. Before the age of seven, children are usually unable to remember the rules they had invented and agreed upon, so they each play according to their own interpretation of the game. Their main concern is not the game itself; what they want is for everyone to enjoy playing together. What a beautiful thought! In a wholesome play environment, children are able to develop better social skills because playing games together requires them to make compromises, to negotiate their roles and the rules, and to learn to lead and to cooperate when being led. And they learn some patience when the game is not being played exactly as they hoped, as well as resilience when they fail to execute well or even lose.

For children, there is also a tremendous therapeutic value in the games they play. It is one of the means for resolving childhood conflicts and traumas. When adults face emotional challenges, we turn to a trusted friend, family member, or even a therapist. Children do not have the intellectual capacity to understand feelings and experiences, so they process them through play. If a child witnesses a violent act, it will often show up in the games he plays. He might repeatedly act out the violence until he is able to resolve the conflict or at least pacify it at the emotional level. If the mother and father fight, upsetting the child, he might reenact this scene through imaginative play. Conflicting feelings and emotions are resolved through the process of play, unless they are so traumatic that the child simply shuts down. A sign of recovery, then, would be the resurgence of play.

Emotional Development and Moral Character

Too many parents feel compelled to replace their child's early years of free play with more structured play and school work at a preschool or kindergarten program, partly out of a belief that children will fall behind academically if they don't start early, learning reading and mathematics.

That is a myth. Child developmental psychologist, Joseph

Chilton Pearce said that at the age of seven, almost to the birthday, a child's intellectual ability to learn increases dramatically and that is when he is ripe for the training of the mind.

Learning to read is the first academic skill a child acquires, being taught in present times sometimes as early as six months to five years of age, yet Mark Van Doren and Mortimer Adler, two great American scholars and reading experts, said that the average age for when a child is ready to read is $6\frac{1}{2}$ to 7 for girls and 7 to $7\frac{1}{2}$ for boys. This is an average, but we know that no child is an average. Each child is ready to learn how to read in his own time, and there are developmental signs for determining when this is.

If you understand the process of learning how to read, then it becomes clear what a waste of time and of childhood it is to force reading on a child before he is developmentally ready.

For example, it will take a five-year-old child a year to learn how to read three-letter words, and even then he will have little, if any, comprehension. In addition, he is too young to decode words, which true reading demands of us, so he simply memorizes what words look like. A child who has reached the age of what Charles Van Doren calls "reading readiness," can learn to read properly in a matter of days or weeks and comprehend and enjoy what he reads.

We should also note that the most successful, innovative and intelligent people in the West today are usually the most prolific readers. When surveyed, it was found that the average CEO reads a book every 10 days, the average engineer reads a book every two to three weeks, and the average surgeon reads a book every three to four weeks.

When we force reading on children before they are developmentally ready, we run the risk of raising children who dislike reading, and therefore, do not read with the obvious consequences such a dislike brings.

In pushing children into formal education too early, we are not only jeopardizing their ability to excel in academic training, which is why in America we keep lowering the educational standards, but we are hindering their emotional development, too. As modern research now knows, a sound emotional development is a prerequisite to developing a strong moral character. "The emotions are, in fact, in charge of the temple of morality," wrote Jonathan Haidt, a psychology professor at the University of Virginia who developed the Moral Foundations Theory. Author and psychologist Daniel Goleman, in his book, *Emotional Intelligence*, demonstrates how a higher degree of emotional intelligence corresponds to a higher sense of morality and is a far greater indicator of a potential for living a successful life, which is exactly what Aristotle taught over two centuries ago.

When we consider the nature of our lives, we see that our daily life is replete with moral choices we must make, starting with arising from our slumber to get up and, for many of us, go to work five days a week. We make moral choices when we honor our commitments and our word even when it is inconvenient to do so; and when we make time to visit the sick or help a neighbor in need. A strong moral fiber which propels us to make the right choices begins first with a strong emotional foundation built during the first seven years of a child's life. It is imperative that we not neglect to place emphasis on a *heart* start for our children. If we do, we run the risk of them not growing up to be compassionate, fulfilled, creative adults.

Consider that children enter this world with what the Greeks referred to as the Four Temperaments. The Four Temperaments are comprised of character and personality archetypes that serve as starting points for character and personality development.

The Four Temperaments include the choleric, phlegmatic, melancholic, and sanguine archetypes. If you have a child who is a predominantly choleric child, he will have a tendency to be bossy, driven, impatient, and ambitious. Phlegmatic children are slow, methodical, reliable, and patient. Melancholics are sensitive, creative, deep-feeling, and artistic; and sanguines are sociable, fun, irresponsible, and flighty.

At birth, a child's "heart" is virtually a blank slate which begins to fill with temperament-driven character and personality traits during the first seven years. Aristotle alluded to this when he said, "Give me a child until he is seven and I will show you the man."

In spite of how well a child is raised, each child will have a God-given nature that will be susceptible to what the Catholics referred to as the Seven Deadly Sins. Most of us will not be able to resist succumbing to these sins in varying proportions, which include pride, envy, anger, sloth, greed, gluttony, and lust, for they are a part of being human. The point then isn't to try to raise our children to be perfect, but to understand that the degree to which we suffer from, and the degree to which we have the ability to avoid these "deadly sins", seems to take root during these first seven years.

Jonathan Haidt, like Aristotle, concluded through his studies on morality that people who live moral lives are happier people. We all want our children to be happy, but we mistake the path to happiness for the need to get a *head* start, when what they need are wholesome childhoods and guidance in developing good character and sound hearts.

Therefore, instead of placing our children in preschool and kindergarten programs before they are emotionally prepared, instead of trying to teach them reading or mathematics long before they are developmentally ready, might it not be better to keep our children home with us, to read beautifully written stories from the past to them, and to let them play as their little hearts so desperately need and desire?

About The Authors

John Taylor Gatto was a schoolteacher for 30 years, winning several awards in the State of New York for his compassionate, insightful, and extraordinary teaching style. Stumbling upon a trail of information that led him to discover the ulterior purpose behind our compulsory educational system, he concluded that schools were in fact dangerous places for children. In protest of what he considered to be a corrupt and incorrigible educational system he gave up his successful and highly acclaimed teaching career and began to speak out about the true purpose behind compulsory schooling. What he uncovered about this topic will not only change how we view modern education but it will even change how we view ourselves. John Taylor Gatto is the author of several books including *The Underground History of American Education*.

Dorothy Leigh Sayers was born at Oxford on 13th June 1893, the only child of the Rev. Henry Sayers, of Anglo-Irish descent. Her father was at the time headmaster of Christ Church Cathedral School, and she was born in the headmaster's house. She was brought up at Bluntisham Rectory, Cambridgeshire, and went to the Godolphin School, Salisbury, where she won a scholarship to Somerville College, Oxford. In 1915 she graduated with first class honors in modern languages. Disliking the routine and seclusion of academic life she joined Blackwell's, the Oxford publishers, worked with her Oxford friend Eric Whelpton at L'École des Roches in Normandy, and from 1922 until 1931 served as copywriter at the London advertising firm of Bensons. She married Arthur Fleming in 1926. In 1928 her father died at Christchurch in the Fens, his last parish, and she bought a cottage at Witham, Essex, to accommodate her mother. On the latter's death a year later she moved in herself and bought the house next door, No. 22 Newland Street, to throw the two houses into one. There she worked until her death in 1957.

She found her culminating role after the war. Dante's writings had long intrigued her. Now she taught herself old Italian and made a translation in terza rima of The Divine Comedy unmatched for its popularity and the clarity of its notes. She also found time to finish her translation of the Song of Roland from the old French. But she unexpectedly died from heart failure on 17 December 1957 while engaged on Dante's third volume, Paradiso, and her friend Dr Barbara Reynolds completed her work. By nature and preference, she was a scholar and an expert on the Middle Ages. To the end she drove herself hard, living the philosophy she expressed in these words: "The only Christian work is good work, well done."

Elizabeth Y. Hanson is a traditional Chinese medicine practitioner turned educator who brings a fresh perspective to the challenges of raising and educating children in the 21st century. Focusing on the "whole" child, including the physical, emotional, neurological, and intellectual development, Elizabeth teaches parents how to raise and educate children capable of reaching their full potential and living successful lives.

The late John Taylor Gatto, award-winning teacher and best-seller author of *Dumbing Us Down*, strongly endorsed Elizabeth as having "mastered current educational difficulties." She is also certified as a Love and Leadership parenting coach by parenting guru John Rosemond.

With her background, training, and 23 years of in-field experience, Elizabeth is uniquely positioned to teach parents her time-tested methods. Her successful homeschooling of her two children, both graduates from one of the top 20 colleges, serves as a testament to the effectiveness of her approach.

Through her online courses, articles, and in-person teaching, she shares her 6-step frameworks for homeschooling brighter, happier, engaged kids who can get into the top 20 colleges and excel personally and professionally.

www.smarthomeschooler.com.